About Skill Builders
Spanish II
Grad

Welcome to Skill Builders *Spanish II* for grades 6–8. This book is designed to help children master essential Spanish vocabulary and concepts through focused practice. This full-color workbook contains grade-level-appropriate activities based on national standards to help ensure that children master important Spanish language skills before progressing.

More than 70 pages of activities cover essential vocabulary and topics, such as adjectives; telling time; and verbs ending in *–ar*, *–er*, and *–ir*. The book's colorful, inviting format and easy-to-follow directions help build children's confidence and make learning Spanish more accessible and enjoyable.

The Skill Builders series offers workbooks that are perfect for keeping children current during the school year or preparing them for the next grade.

carsondellosa.com
Carson-Dellosa Publishing, LLC
Greensboro, North Carolina

Printed in the USA • All rights reserved.
ISBN 978-1-936023-37-0
06-214161151

Contenido (Table of Contents)

Los números (Numbers)

Escribe con palabras los números en español. (Write the numbers in Spanish using words.)

51 _____ 52 _____

53 _____ 54 _____

55 _____ 56 _____

57 _____ 58 _____

59 _____ 60 _____

61 _____ 62 _____

63 _____ 64 _____

65 _____ 66 _____

Los números (Numbers)

Escribe con palabras los números en español. (Write the numbers in Spanish using words.)

67

68

_____

69

70
setenta

_____

75

80
ochenta

_____

85

90
noventa

_____

95

100
cien

_____

101
ciento uno

200
doscientos

_____

201

300
trescientos

_____

303	400 cuatrocientos
404	500 quinientos
600 seiscientos	700 setecientos
800 ochocientos	900 novecientos
1,000 mil	1,100 mil cien
1,500 mil quinientos	2,000 dos mil
10,000 diez mil	100,000 cien mil
1,000,000 un millón	2,000,000 dos millones

Note: Ciento/s changes to cienta/s when used with feminine nouns.

Ejemplos (Examples): doscient**os** chicos

doscient**as** chicas

Práctica con los números
(Practice: Numbers)

Escribe con palabras los números en español. (Write the numbers in Spanish in words.)

67 _____

181 _____

92 _____

74 _____

243 _____

515 _____

926 _____

304 _____

1,200 _____

4,000 _____

500,126 _____

1,894,037 _____

3,600,012 _____

987,651 _____

Escribe los númeroscon dígitos. (Write the numbers using digits.)

trescientos noventa y tres _____

cincuenta y cuatro _____

ocho mil siete _____

mil ciento uno _____

setecientos trece _____

dos mil once _____

un millón catorce _____

novecientos dos _____

quinientos _____

quince mil _____

un millón seiscientos _____

diez mil veintidós _____

setecientos treinta _____

catorce millones _____

cinco mil quinientos _____

¿Cuánto? (How much?)

Escribe el problema y da la respuesta en español.
(Write each problem and give the answer in Spanish.)

Ejemplo (Example): mil seiscientos once   1,611
                     + dos mil doscientos   + 2,200
                        tres mil ochocientos once   3,811

1.   quinientos treinta y uno   _____

   + novecientos catorce   + _____

      _____   _____

2.   setecientos ochenta   _____

   + mil ochocientos uno   + _____

      _____   _____

3.   cuatro mil seiscientos   _____

   − cuatrocientos seis   − _____

      _____   _____

4.   diez mil ciento diecisiete   _____

   + mil quinientos setenta   + _____

      _____   _____

Escribe cómo dirías los años siguientes en español.

(Write how you would say the following years in Spanish.)

Ejemplo (Example): 2010 – **dos mil diez**

1492 _____

_____

1776 _____

_____

1955 _____

_____

1812 _____

_____

1548 _____

_____

1637 _____

_____

Los verbos que terminan en –ar (Verbs That End in –ar)

Estudia la lista de verbos a continuación. (Study the list of verbs below.)

hablar = to speak
cantar = to sing
nadar = to swim
escuchar = to listen (to)
bailar = to dance
estudiar = to study

comprar = to buy
trabajar = to work
preparar = to prepare
caminar = to walk
desear = to want
llevar = to wear

llorar = to cry
tocar = to play
visitar = to visit
saludar = to greet
mirar = to look (at)
contestar = to answer

Conjuga los verbos de acuerdo al ejemplo.

(Conjugate the verbs according to the example.)

verb – hablar   **stem** – habl-

yo hablo   nosotros/as hablamos

tú hablas

usted ⎫
él   ⎬ habla
ella ⎭

ustedes ⎫
ellos   ⎬ hablan
ellas   ⎭

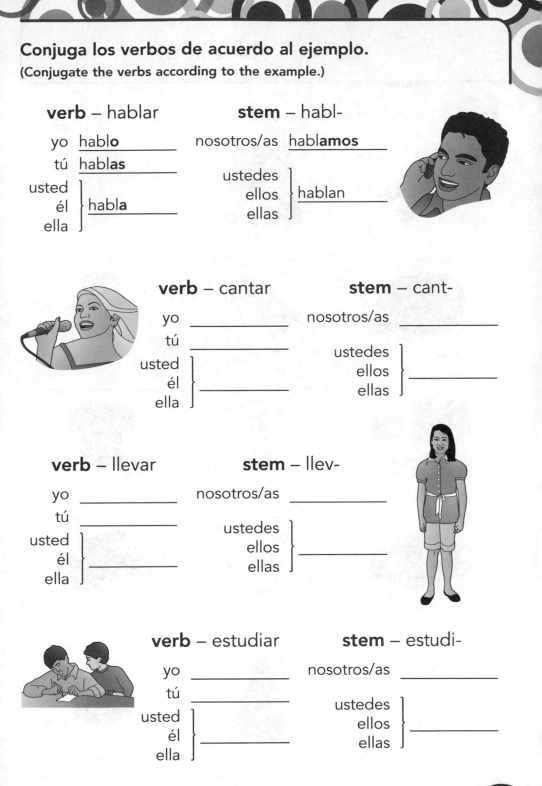

verb – cantar   **stem** – cant-

yo _____   nosotros/as _____

tú _____

usted ⎫
él   ⎬ _____
ella ⎭

ustedes ⎫
ellos   ⎬ _____
ellas   ⎭

verb – llevar   **stem** – llev-

yo _____   nosotros/as _____

tú _____

usted ⎫
él   ⎬ _____
ella ⎭

ustedes ⎫
ellos   ⎬ _____
ellas   ⎭

verb – estudiar   **stem** – estudi-

yo _____   nosotros/as _____

tú _____

usted ⎫
él   ⎬ _____
ella ⎭

ustedes ⎫
ellos   ⎬ _____
ellas   ⎭

La ropa (Clothing)

Escribe las palabras en español. (Write the words in Spanish.)

_____

_____

_____

_____

_____

_____

_____

_____

_____

_____

_____

_____

_____

_____

_____

Escribe las frases en español. (Write the sentences in Spanish.)

1. I like T-shirts

   _____

2. Marcos wears shorts.

   _____

3. Ana and María wear dresses.

   _____

4. We wear swimsuits.

   _____

5. I buy the tie.

   _____

6. Do you like to wear sandals?

   _____

7. They wear pants.

   _____

8. They buy skirts.

   _____

9. She is buying a coat.

   _____

10. He wears a jacket.

    _____

11. I like sweaters.

    _____

¿Qué? (What?)

Qué is the question word meaning *what*. To form a question using *qué* follow this pattern:

¿Qué + verb + subject?

The answer to this type of question will always be a noun.

Ejemplo 1 (Example 1):

¿**Qué** compras tú?
(What are you buying?)

Yo compro **una camisa**.
        (noun)
(I'm buying a shirt.)

¿**Qué** admiran ustedes?
(What do you admire?)

Nosotros admiramos el **barco**.
(We admire the boat.)

Ejemplo 2 (Example 2):

¿**Qué** juega ella?
(What is she playing?)

Ella juega al **fútbol**. (noun)
(She plays soccer.)

Note that the verb has to agree with the subject pronoun. Remember that a question asked of *tú* or *usted* should be answered with *yo*, and a question asked of *ustedes* should be answered with *nosotros* or *nosotras*.

Usa los dibujos para contestar las preguntas siguientes en español. (Use the pictures to answer the following questions in Spanish.)

1. ¿Qué mira él?

_____

2. ¿Qué estudias tú?

_____

3. ¿Qué cantan ellas?

_____

4. ¿Qué lleva ella?

_____

5. ¿Qué toca usted?

_____

6. ¿Qué escuchan ustedes?

_____

7. ¿Qué compra Manuel?

_____

8. ¿Qué deseas tú?

_____

9. ¿Qué habla él?

_____

10. ¿Qué prepara Carlota?

_____

Las preguntas con qué
(Questions with *Qué*)

Escribe las preguntas usando qué. (Write questions using *qué*.)

1. ¿ <u>Qué te gusta</u> ?
   Me gusta el helado.

2. ¿ ———————————————— ?
   Ella compra una falda.

3. ¿ ———————————————— ?
   Él habla ingles.

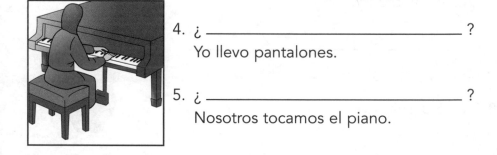

4. ¿ ———————————————— ?
   Yo llevo pantalones.

5. ¿ ———————————————— ?
   Nosotros tocamos el piano.

6. ¿ ———————————————— ?
   Yo estudio historia.

7. ¿ ———————————————— ?
   Nosotros visitamos México.

8. ¿ ———————————————— ?
   Él escucha la música.

9. ¿ —————————————— ?
Ellos cantan la canción.

10. ¿ —————————————— ?
Yo miro el televisor.

11. ¿ —————————————— ?
Ellas contestan la pregunta.

12. ¿ —————————————— ?
Me gusta el español.

13. ¿ —————————————— ?
Ella estudia matemáticas.

14. ¿ —————————————— ?
Nosotros compramos uvas.

15. ¿ —————————————— ?
Ella toca la guitarra.

Las preguntas: ¿sí o no?
(Yes/No Questions)

To form a yes/no question, reverse the order of the subject and the verb.

Ejemplos (Examples):

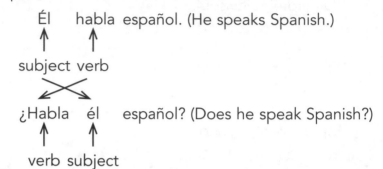

Él   habla español. (He speaks Spanish.)

subject verb

¿Habla   él   español? (Does he speak Spanish?)

verb subject

Contesta las siguientes preguntas. (Answer the following questions.)

1. ¿Habla ella inglés?

   Sí, _____

2. ¿Cantan ellos bien?

   No, _____

3. ¿Nadan ustedes en la piscina?

   Sí, _____

4. ¿Llevan ellas vestidos?

   Sí, _____

5. ¿Estudias tú historia?

No, _____

6. ¿Prepara ella la comida?

Sí, _____

7. ¿Miran ustedes el televisor?

No, _____

8. ¿Escucha usted la radio?

Sí, _____

9. ¿Baila él bien?

No, _____

10. ¿Llora ella?

Sí, _____

11. ¿Compra usted el suéter?

Sí, _____

Las preguntas: ¿sí o no?
(Yes/No Questions)

Escribe las preguntas. (Write the questions.)

1. ¿ _____ ?
   Sí, yo bailo mucho.

2. ¿ _____ ?
   No, ella no nada bien.

3. ¿ _____ ?
   Sí, nosotros caminamos.

4. ¿ _____ ?
   No, él no habla francés.

5. ¿ _____ ?
   Sí, ellas escuchan la radio.

6. ¿ _____ ?
   No, yo no toco la guitarra.

7. ¿ _____ ?
   Sí, nosotros visitamos España.

8. ¿ _____ ?
   No, ella no lleva abrigo.

9. ¿ _____ ?
   Sí, yo estudio ciencias (science).

10. ¿ _____ ?
    No, ellos no bailan.

11. ¿ _____ ?
    Sí, yo hablo español.

12. ¿ _____ ?
    No, él no mira el televisor.

Práctica de las preguntas
(Practice: Questions)

Contesta las preguntas según los dibujos.
(Answer the questions according to the pictures.)

1. ¿Hablas tú ingles?

_____

2. ¿Qué habla él?

_____

3. ¿Miran ellas el televisor?

_____

4. ¿Qué te gusta?

_____

5. ¿Nada usted?

_____

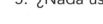

6. ¿Escuchan ustedes la radio?

_____

7. ¿Llora ella?

_____

8. ¿Qué tocas tú?

_____

9. ¿Cantan ellas?

_____

10. ¿Saludan ellos?

_____

11. ¿Qué estudia ella?

_____

Los adjetivos (Adjectives)

An **adjective** is a word that describes a noun. In Spanish **all nouns have gender**. They are either masculine or feminine. Each adjective **must agree** with the **gender** of the noun it describes. The adjectives in Spanish have both masculine and feminine forms. Use the form that agrees with the gender of the noun.

For adjectives ending in **–o** in the masculine form, change the **–o** to **–a** to get the feminine form.

Ejemplo (Example):

masculine	feminine	
alto	alta	(tall)
bajo	baja	(short)
bonito	bonita	(pretty)
aburrido	aburrida	(boring)

Escribe el femenino de cada adjetivo a continuación.
(Write the feminine forms of each adjective below.)

1. **serio** _____
   (serious)

2. **gracioso** _____
   (funny)

3. **moreno** _____
   (dark haired)

4. **rubio** _____
   (blond)

5. **viejo** _____
   (old)

6. **tímido** _____
   (shy)

7. **pequeño** _____
   (small)

8. **simpático** _____
   (nice)

9. **antipático** _____
   (not nice, mean)

Los adjetivos (Adjectives)

Most adjectives ending in **–e** or a **consonant** remain the same for both masculine and feminine forms.

Masculine	Feminine

Ejemplos (Examples): inteligente ⟶ inteligente (smart)

fácil ⟶ fácil (easy)

Here are several adjectives of this type:

excelente = excellent

grande = big

difícil = difficult

independiente = independent

paciente = patient

impaciente = impatient

interesante = interesting

inocente = innocent

joven = young

Note: Adjectives generally come **after** the nouns they describe in Spanish.

Ejemplos (Examples):   an **easy** test = un examen **fácil**

a **tall** girl = una chica **alta**

Completa los espacios en blanco con la forma correcta del adjetivo subrayado de cada oración. (Fill in the blanks with the correct form of the underlined adjective in each phrase.)

Remember: Some adjectives change form because of gender.

1. a <u>smart</u> man = **un hombre** _____

2. a <u>young</u> woman = **una mujer** _____

3. a <u>big</u> car = **un carro** _____

4. a <u>serious</u> boy = **un chico** _____

5. a <u>dark-haired</u> girl = **una chica** _____

6. an <u>innocent</u> child = **un niño** _____

7. a <u>patient</u> mother = **una madre** _____

8. an <u>independent</u> country = **un país** _____

9. a <u>short</u> boy = **un chico** _____

10. a <u>blond</u> teacher = **una maestra** _____

11. a <u>shy</u> cat= **un gato** _____

12. an <u>interesting</u> class = **una clase** _____

13. an <u>excellent</u> movie theater = **un cine** _____

14. a <u>difficult</u> test = **un examen** _____

15. a <u>big</u> house = **una casa** _____

16. a <u>funny</u> frog = **una rana** _____

Los adjetivos (Adjectives)

Adjectives in Spanish must agree in **number** as well as **gender**. That is, if the noun is singular, then the adjective describing it must also be singular. If the noun is plural, then the adjective must also be plural.

To make an adjective plural
1. add **–s** if it ends in a vowel.
    Ejemplo (Example):   alto ⟶ altos
                    grande ⟶ grandes
2. add **–es** if it ends in a consonant.
    Ejemplo (Example):   fácil ⟶ fáciles

Most adjectives have four forms.

	singular	plural
masculine	alto	altos
feminine	alta	altas

If a group contains both masculine and feminine nouns, use the masculine form.
    Ejemplo (Example):   Los chicos y las chicas son alt**os**.
                    (The boys and the girls are tall.)

Completa los espacios en blanco con la forma correcta de los adjetivos subrayados. (Fill in the blanks with the correct forms of the underlined adjectives.)

1. <u>small</u> girls = **las chicas** _____

2. <u>interesting</u> books = **los libros** _____

3. <u>shy</u> men = **los hombres** _____

4. <u>innocent</u> people = **las personas** _____

5. <u>difficult</u> tests = **los exámenes** _____

6. <u>boring</u> classes = **las clases** _____

7. <u>pretty</u> flowers = **las flores** _____

8. <u>excellent</u> teachers = **los maestros** _____

9. <u>funny</u> photos = **las fotos** _____

10. <u>big</u> meals = **las comidas** _____

11. <u>nice</u> boys = **los chicos** _____

12. <u>impatient</u> parents= **los padres** _____

Práctica con adjetivos
(Practice: Adjectives)

Escribe la forma correcta de los adjetivos.
(Write the correct form of the adjectives.)

1. (big) **una casa** _____

2. (short) **un hombre** _____

3. (blond) **una chica** _____

4. (boring) **una maestra** _____

5. (small) **una clase** _____

6. (excellent) **un libro** _____

7. (tall) **un elefante** _____

8. (nice) **unas cebras** _____

9. (mean) **unos monos** _____

10. (old) **una casa** _____

11. (funny) **un perro** _____

12. (dark-haired) **un niño** _____

13. (young) **un chico** _____

14. (nice) **una chica** _____

15. (smart) **unos chicos** _____

16. (difficult) **un problema** _____

17. (innocent) **unos estudiantes** _____

18. (easy) **unos exámenes** _____

19. (patient) **una tortuga** _____

20. (smart) **un conejo** _____

21. (big) **unos árboles** _____

22. (nice) **un maestro** _____

23. (tall) **unas chicas** _____

24. (blond) **un hombre** _____

El verbo: ser (The Verb: *To Be*)

The verb **ser** (to be) is used with adjectives to describe people or things. *Ser* does not follow a regular pattern like the **–ar** verbs. It is an irregular verb.

Note its forms.

Ser

yo soy		**nosotros/as** somos	
tú eres			
usted		**ustedes**	
él	es	**ellos**	son
ella		**ellas**	

Conjuga el verbo ser con el adjetivo alto.

(Conjugate he verb ser with the adjective alto (tall).)

1. Yo _____ _____.

2. Tú _____ _____. (feminine)

3. Usted _____ _____. (masculine)

4. Él _____ _____.

5. Ella _____ _____.

6. Nosotros _____ _____.

7. Nosotras _____ _____.

8. Ustedes _____ _____. (masculine)

9. Ellos _____ _____.

10. Ellas _____ _____.

Conjuga el verbo ser con los siguientes adjetivos.
(Conjugate the verb ser with the following adjectives.)

bajo (short)

1. Yo _____ _____.

2. Tú _____ _____. (masculine)

3. Ella _____ _____.

4. Nosotros _____ _____.

5. Ellos _____ _____.

6. Ustedes _____ _____. (feminine)

inteligente (intelligent)

1. Tú _____ _____.

2. Ellas _____ _____.

3. Nosotros _____ _____.

4. Yo _____ _____.

5. Ustedes _____ _____.

6. Él _____ _____.

7. Ellos _____ _____.

8. Usted _____ _____.

El verbo: ser (The Verb: To Be)

Use the adjectives to describe the people and things listed. All adjectives are given in the masculine singular form. Be sure to make them agree!

1. Mónica – inteligente , simpático

   _____

   _____

2. Roberto – inocente, alto

   _____

   _____

3. Ana y María – paciente, rubio

   _____

   _____

4. Marcos y Pablo – joven, impaciente

   _____

   _____

5. Pedro y Rosita – bajo, moreno

   _____

   _____

6. Los libros – fácil, interesante

_____

_____

7. Nosotros – gracioso, independiente

_____

_____

8. Yo (feminine) – alto, simpático

_____

_____

9. La chica – antipático, aburrido

_____

_____

10. Las casas – bonito, pequeño

_____

_____

Las preguntas con el verbo ser
(Questions Using The Verb *To Be*)

Contesta las preguntas. Usa los dibujos como pistas para tus respuestas. No te olvides de la concordancia de los adejtivos. (Answer the questions. Use the pictures as clues for your answers. Don't forget the agreement of the adjectives.)

Ejemplos (Examples):

¿Es Mario rubio?

Sí, él es rubio.

¿Es Eduardo antipático?

No, él no es antipático.

Él es simpático.
(nice)

1. ¿Es la maestra estricta (strict)?

_____

2. ¿Eres tú bajo?

_____

(tall) _____

3. ¿Son los monos graciosos?

   _____

4. ¿Son ustedes pacientes?

   _____

5. ¿Es Rosita morena?

   _____

   (blond) _____

6. ¿Es el libro interesante?

   _____

   (boring) _____

7. ¿Es Alberto viejo?

   _____

   (young) _____

8. ¿Es Juana simpática?

   _____

   (mean) _____

Las profesiones (Professions)

The names of some professions have different masculine and feminine forms. Those that end in **–o** usually change the **–o** to **–a** to form the feminine.

Ejemplo (Example):   un maestro (m)   una maestra (f)
(a grade school teacher)

Those that end in **–e** or **–a** remain the same in both forms.

Ejemplo (Example):   un cantante (m)   una cantante (f)
(a singer)

                          un artista (m)   una artista (f)
(an artist)

Some do not follow a special pattern, but have different forms for masculine and feminine.

Ejemplos (Examples):   un actor (m)   una actriz (f)
(an actor)   (an actress)

                            un profesor (m)   una profesora (f)
(a high school teacher)

                            un doctor (m)   una doctora (f)
(a doctor)

These are examples of professions.

una enfermera = a nurse

una secretaria = a secretary

un ingeniero = an engineer

un abogado = a lawyer

un mecánico = a mechanic

un técnico = a technician

un piloto = a pilot

un cocinero = a cook

un fotógrafo = a photographer

un músico = a musician

un dentista = a dentist

un periodista = a journalist

un gerente = a manager

un agricultor = a farmer

un obrero = a factory worker

un escritor = a writer

un poeta = a poet

un bailarín = a dancer (m)

una bailarina = a dancer (f)

El verbo ser con las profesiones (Professions with the Verb *To Be*)

The indefinite articles un, una (a/an) are not used with the professions after the verb ser unless they are modified by an adjective.

Ejemplos (Examples):   Gloria es cantante.
(Gloria is a singer.)

Gloria es una buena cantante.
(Gloria is a good singer.)

Llena los espacios en blanco con la forma correcta de ser y las profesiones indicadas. (Fill in the blanks with the correct form of ser and the indicated professions.)

1. Yo _____ _____.
(artist)

2. Manuel _____ _____.
(mechanic)

3. Nosotros _____ _____.
(journalist)

4. Anita _____ _____.
(nurse)

5. El señor González _____ _____.
(musician)

6. Maria _____.
   (singer)

7. Mark Twain _____ _____.
   (writer)

8. Mi mamá _____ _____.
   (doctor)

9. Mi papá _____ _____.
   (pilot)

10. Usted _____ _____.
    (cook)

11. Patricia _____ _____.
    (dentist)

12. Tú _____ _____.
    (photographer)

13. Ellos _____ _____.
    (lawyer)

14. José _____ _____.
    (dancer)

15. Ella _____ _____.
    (teacher)

La hora (Telling Time)

To answer **¿Qué hora es?** (What time is it?), follow the patterns below.

Escribe las horas de los relojes.
(Write the times shown on the clocks.)

Es la una.

_____

Son las dos.

_____

Son las tres.

_____

Son las cuatro.

_____

Es mediodía.

_____

Es medianoche.

_____

Son las cinco y cinco.

_____

Son las ocho y cuarto.

_____

Son las diez y veinticinco.

_____

Escribe las horas de los relojes.
(Write the times shown on the clocks.)

Son las nueve y media.

_____

Son las diez menos veinte.

_____

Son las diez menos cuarto.

_____

Son las diez menos diez.

_____

Son las diez menos cinco.

_____

La hora (Telling Time)

The preposition *a* is used to tell at what time something will take place.

Ejemplos (Examples): ¿A qué hora es la clase de español?
(At what time is the Spanish class?)

La clase es a las ocho.
(The class is at eight o'clock.)

To be more specific about the time use…

de la mañana = in the morning/A.M.

de la tarde = in the afternoon/P.M.

de la noche = in the evening/P.M.

Mira el horario y contesta las preguntas. Recuerda escribir de la mañana o de la tarde. (Look at the schedule and answer the questions. Be sure to include *de la mañana* or *de la tarde*.)

Nombre: *María Molina*

8:00–8:55 historia

9:00–9:55 inglés

10:00–11:15 recreo

10:20–11:15 geografía

11:20–12:20 almuerzo

12:30–1:25 arte

1:30–2:25 matemáticas

1. ¿A qué hora es la clase de inglés?

   _____ .

2. ¿A qué hora es el almuerzo?

   _____ .

3. ¿A qué hora es la clase de geografía?

   _____ .

4. ¿A qué hora es la clase de arte?

   _____ .

5. ¿A qué hora es el recreo?

   _____ .

6. ¿A qué hora es la clase de matemáticas?

   _____ .

7. ¿A qué hora es la clase de historia?

   _____ .

8. ¿A qué hora terminan las clases?

   _____ .

El verbo: estar (The Verb: *To Be*)

You have already learned the verb **ser** (to be). In Spanish there is another verb, **estar** which also means "to be." Study its forms below.

Estar

yo estoy		**nosotros/as** estamos	
tú estás			
usted		**ustedes**	
él } está		**ellos** } están	
ella		**ellas**	

Ser and **estar** are not interchangeable. **Ser** is used to identify or describe. It tells what something is, its basic characteristics, or its **origin**.

Ejemplos (Examples): Manuel **es** maestro. (Manuel is a teacher.)
(identfies who he is)

Manuel **es** alto (Manuel is tall.)
(describes him)

Manuel **es** de California. (Manuel is from California.)
(tells where he's from)

Estar is used to tell the location of something or how someone feels.

Ejemplos (Examples): Manuel **está** en la casa. (Manuel is at home.)
(tells where he is)

Manuel **está** triste. (Manuel is sad.)
(tells how he feels)

Llena los espacios en blanco con la forma correcta de estar.
(Fill in the blanks with the correct forms of estar.)

1. Nosotras _____ en Nueva York.

2. Ellos _____ tristes (sad).

3. Yo no _____ listo (ready).

4. ¿_____ tú contento (happy)?

5. Susana _____ en la escuela hoy.

Decide si usar el verbo ser o estar y llena los espacios en blanco con la forma correcta. (Decide whether to use the verb ser or estar and fill in the blanks with the correct forms.)

1. Ella _____ de Florida.

2. Nosotros _____ inteligentes.

3. Miguel y Ana _____ en la playa.

4. Mi papá _____ moreno.

5. La familia _____ en México.

6. Yo _____ en España.

7. Tú no _____ contenta.

8. Ustedes _____ en la piscina.

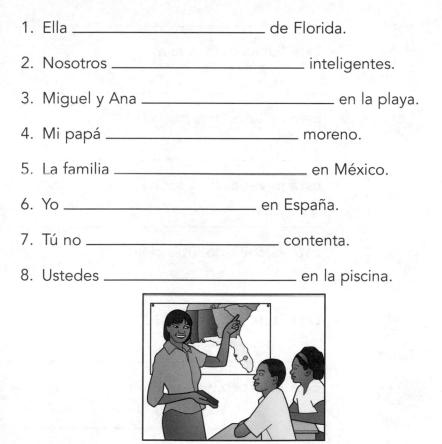

El tiempo (The weather)

The verb *estar* can also be used to talk about the weather.

Ejemplos (Examples): ¿Cómo está el tiempo?   Está nublado.
(How's the weather like?)   (It is cloudy.)

Escribe las siguientes expresiones sobre el tiempo en español. (Write the following expressions about the weather in Spanish.)

 Está soleado. (It is sunny.)

_____

 Está nublado. (It is cloudy.)

_____

 Está lluvioso. (It is rainy.)

_____

 Está helado. (It is frosty.)

_____

 Está nevado. (It is snowy.)

_____

 Está despejado. (It is clear.)

_____

 Está fresco. (It is cool.)

_____

 Está caluroso. (It is warm.)

_____

Contesta las preguntas usando los dibujos.

(Answer the questions using the pictures.)

 1. ¿Cómo está el tiempo?

_____

 2. ¿Cómo está el tiempo?

_____

 3. ¿Cómo está el tiempo?

_____

 4. ¿Cómo está el tiempo?

_____

 5. ¿Cómo está el tiempo?

_____

 6. ¿Cómo está el tiempo?

_____

 7. ¿Cómo está el tiempo?

_____

 8. ¿Cómo está el tiempo?

_____

¿Dónde? (Where?)

en el campo

en la ciudad

en la escuela

en el restaurante

en la playa

en el aeropuerto

en la piscina

en la casa

en el cine

en la oficina

en España

en el teatro

en los Estados Unidos

en México

¿Dónde? (Where?)

Contesta las preguntas de acuerdo a los dibujos.
(Answer the questions according to the pictures.)

1. ¿Dónde está Cecilia?

_____

2. ¿Dónde está Juan?

_____

3. ¿Dónde estás tú?

_____

4. ¿Dónde están ellos?

_____

5. ¿Dónde está usted?

_____

6. ¿Dónde están ustedes?

_____

7. ¿Dónde nadan José y Adela?

_____

8. ¿Dónde trabaja Marta?

_____

9. ¿Dónde están los chicos?

_____

10. ¿Dónde estudias tú?

_____

11. ¿Dónde están los actores?

_____

12. ¿Dónde está el avión?

_____

El verbo: ir (The Verb: *To Go*)

The verb *ir* (to go) is another irregular verb. Study its form below.

Ir

yo	voy	**nosotros/as**	vamos
tú	vas		
usted		**ustedes**	
él	va	**ellos**	van
ella		**ellas**	

Ir is usually followed by **a** (to). Note that when **a** is followed by **el** (the), the two combine to form **al**.

A combines with **¿dónde?** to form **¿adónde?** to ask where someone is going.

Here are some places you might go.

la biblioteca = the library
el café = the café
el museo = the museum
la escuela = the school
el parque = the park
el hotel = the hotel
la estación = the train station

Contesta las preguntas siguientes usando *ir a* y el lugar del dibujo. (Answer the following questions using *ir a* and the place in the picture.)

1. ¿Adónde vas tú?

_____

2. ¿Adónde va Juan?

_____

3. ¿Adónde van Rosita y Carlos?

_____

4. ¿Adónde van ustedes?

_____

5. ¿Adónde van los turistas?

_____

6. ¿Adónde va usted?

_____

7. ¿Adónde va Fernando?

_____

8. ¿Adónde va Carlota?

_____

El verbo: ir (The Verb: To Go)

Ir is followed by **a + an infinitive** to tell what is going to happen in the future.

Ejemplo (Example): Yo **voy a viajar** mañana.
(I'm going to travel tomorrow.)

Tell what the following people are going to do tomorrow by combining the given elements.

Ejemplo (Example): **Adán/trabajar**
Adán va a trabajar mañana.
(Adán is going to work tomorrow.)

1. Lola/cantar

_____

2. Cristina y Ana/bailar

_____

3. Los chicos/estudiar

_____

4. Yo/caminar

_____

5. Nosotros/contestar

_____

6. Las hermanas/visitar

_____

7. Manuel/trabajar

_____

If you make a negative sentence that uses two verbs, be sure to put *no* before the first verb.

Ejemplo (Example): No, yo no voy a cantar.
(No, I'm not going to sing.)

Contesta las preguntas en español.

(Answer the questions in Spanish.)

1. ¿Vas a estudiar tú mañana?

   Sí, _____.

2. ¿Van a llorar las chicas?

   Sí, _____.

3. ¿Van a hablar ustedes en clase?

   Sí, _____.

4. ¿Va a escuchar ella?

   Sí, _____.

5. ¿Va a mirar el televisor él?

   Sí, _____.

6. ¿Va a comprar ropa usted?

   Sí, _____.

7. ¿Vas a nadar tú mañana?

   Sí, _____.

Los verbos que terminan en –er (Verbs That End in –er)

Verbs that end in **–er** follow a regular pattern like the verbs that end in **–ar**. Take off the **–er** and add the following endings:

yo	–o	**nosotros/as**	–emos
tú	–es		
usted		**ustedes**	
él	}–e	**ellos**	}–en
ella		**ellas**	

Some **–er** verbs that follow this pattern are:

comer = to eat
beber = to drink
deber = to owe
vender = to sell
creer = to believe
comprender = to understand
correr = to run
aprender = to learn
leer = to read

Conjugate the verb **comer**.

stem _____

yo _____   nosotros/as _____

tú _____

usted ⎫
él   ⎬ _____
ella ⎭

ustedes ⎫
ellos ⎬ _____
ellas ⎭

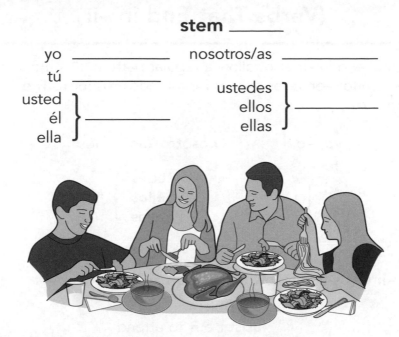

Escribe las formas correctas de los verbos entre paréntesis.
(Write the correct forms of the verbs in parenthesis.)

1. (**beber**) Nosotros _____ el refresco.

2. (**vender**) La chica _____ ropa.

3. (**aprender**) Los estudiantes _____.

4. (**correr**) David _____ muy rápido.

5. (**comprender**) ¿ _____ustedes?

6. (**deber**) Yo _____ cincuenta pesos.

7. (**comer**) ¿_____ tú mucho?

8. (**saber**) Ella no _____ la respuesta.

9. (**leer**) Usted _____ el libro.

10. (**beber**) Yo _____ café.

Los verbos que terminan en –ir
(Verbs That End in –ir)

Verbs that end in **–ir** also follow a regular pattern. It is the same as the pattern for **–er** verbs except for the *nosotros* form. The **–ir** verb endings are:

yo –o   **nosotros/as** –imos

tú –es

usted
él } –e   **ustedes**
ella   **ellos** } –en
                     ellas

Some **–ir** verbs that follow this pattern are:

escribir = to write
asistir a = to attend
decidir = to decide
subir = to go up
recibir = to receive
vivir = to live
cumplir años = to have a birthday

Conjuga el verbo escribir. (Conjugate the verb escribir.)

stem _____

yo _____ nosotros/as _____

tú _____

usted
él } _____

ella

ustedes
ellos } _____

ellas

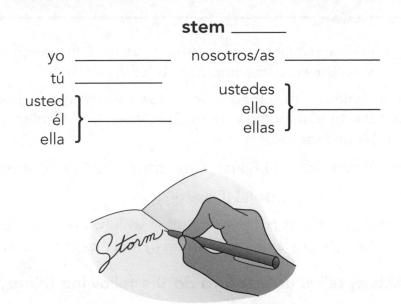

Escribe las formas correctas de los verbos entre paréntesis.
(Write the correct forms of the verbs in parentheses.)

1. (**decidir**) Ella no _____ rápidamente.

2. (**vivir**) ¿_____ ustedes en México?

3. (**abrir**) El cine _____ a las diez.

4. (**recibir**) Yo _____ buenas calificaciones.

5. (**asistir**) Nosotros _____ a la escuela.

6. (**cumplir**) Eduardo _____ años hoy.

7. (**subir**) ¿_____ tú las escaleras (stairs)?

8. (**escribir**) J. K. Rowling _____ libros.

9. (**abrir**) ¿_____ usted la puerta (door)?

10. (**cumplir**) Ellos _____ siete años.

El imperativo (The Imperative)

When you tell someone to do something, you use the command form of a verb known as the **imperative** (el imperativo).

To give a command to someone you know well using a regular verb, use the **tú** form of the verb minus the **–s**. As in English, the "you" (tú) is understood.

Ejemplo (Example):   **Tú bailas.** (You dance. You are dancing.)

   ¡Baila! (Dance!)

Notice that commands are always written with two exclamation marks in Spanish, one at the beginning (¡) and one at the end (!).

To practice, tell your friend to do the following things.

Sing! _____

Speak Spanish! _____

Watch television! _____

Swim! _____

Eat! _____

Listen! _____

Run! _____

Answer! _____

To give a command to someone you address as **usted**, use the **yo** form of the verb. Drop the final **o** and add the opposite vowel ending. (**–ar** commands end in **–e**, **–er** commands end in **–a**)

Ejemplo (Example): **Usted baila.** (You dance. You are dancing.)

¡Baile! (Dance!)

To practice, tell your older neighbor to do the following things.

Sing! _____

Speak Spanish! _____

Watch television! _____

Swim! _____

Eat! _____

Listen! _____

Run! _____

Answer! _____

Anita

Lee el párrafo y contesta las preguntas.
(Read the paragraph and answer the questions.)

Anita vive en Santiago. Ella es de Chile. Ella
habla español y habla inglés también. Le
gusta la clase de inglés de la escuela. Ella es
muy inteligente, pero no le gusta la maestra
de biología. Le gusta mucho la clase de
geografía. Le gusta llevar una camiseta y unos
jeans a la escuela. Le gusta cantar y bailar.

1. ¿Dónde vive Anita?

   _____

   _____

2. ¿Es Anita de México?

   _____

3. ¿Qué clases le gustan a Anita?

   _____

4. ¿Que le gusta llevar a la escuela?

   _____

5. ¿Habla Anita francés?

   _____

Pablo

Lee el párrafo y contesta las preguntas.
(Read the paragraph and answer the questions.)

Pablo es muy deportivo. Le gusta el fútbol. Él
es alto, rubio y simpático. Él trabaja con su tío.
Le gusta la escuela, las clases y los maestros.
Le gustan los estudiantes. Pablo y sus amigos
escuchan la radio y miran el televisor.

1. ¿Es Pablo deportivo?

   _____

   _____

2. ¿Es Pablo bajo y moreno?

   _____

   _____

3. ¿Estudia él con sus amigos?

   _____

   _____

4. ¿Le gusta la escuela?

   _____

   _____

Mónica y Carlos (Mónica and Carlos)

Lee el párrafo y contesta las preguntas.
(Read the paragraphs and answer the questions.)

¡Hola! Me llamo Mónica Sánchez. Yo soy de España. Yo soy la amiga (friend) de Carlos Molina.

Carlos es de los Estados Unidos. Carlos es fantástico. Él es bajo, rubio y sincero. Le gustan los deportes. A mí también. Nos gusta el tenis y el fútbol. No nos gusta nadar o correr.

Yo soy estudiante de una escuela en Barcelona. Carlos es estudiante de una escuela en Tarragona, me gusta la clase de historia y me gustan mucho las matemáticas. A Carlos no le gustan las matemáticas pero a él gusta la clase de historia también. Nosotros somos inteligentes.

1. ¿Es Mónica de los Estados Unidos?

   _____

   _____

2. ¿Es Carlos de España?

   _____

   _____

3. ¿Como es Carlos?

_____

4. ¿A Carlos le gustan los deportes?

_____

5. ¿A Mónica también le gustan los deportes?

_____

6. ¿A ellos les gusta correr?

_____

7. ¿Donde está la escuela de Mónica?

_____

8. ¿Donde está la escuela de Carlos?

_____

9. ¿A Mónica le gusta la historia?

_____

10. ¿Son ellos inteligentes?

_____

Un repaso (A review)

Usa las pistas para resolver el crucigrama.
(Use the clues to solve the crossword puzzle.)

Across

5. where **en español**
6. worn in cold weather
7. **yo** form of **ir**
8. opposite of **correr**
10. **se habla en España**
11. opposite of **alta**
13. **yo** form of **estar**
14. opposite of **joven**
16. opposite of **antipático**
18. **tú** form of **escribir**

Down

1. **donde trabajan los actores**
2. to live
3. **yo** form of **ser**
4. **donde vamos a nadar**
5. 200 **en español**
9. **él trabaja en un avión**
12. **nosotros** form of **ser**
15. worn by girls
17. **veinte + ochenta**
19. to go

Escribe las palabras siguientes en español.
(Write the following words in Spanish.)

1. to be _____

2. boring (masculine, singular) _____

3. to cry _____

4. easy (singular) _____

5. factory worker (masculine, plural) _____

6. serious (feminine, singular) _____

7. to greet _____

8. journalist _____

9. lawyer (masculine, plural) _____

10. midnight _____

11. nurse (feminine, singular) _____

12. to open _____

13. to read _____

14. funny (masculine, singular) _____

15. sandals _____

16. shoes _____

17. sixty _____

18. tie _____

19. what _____

20. to work _____

Un repaso (A review)

Escoge un verbo de la lista y escríbelo en su forma correcta en la oración.

(Choose a verb from the list and write it in the correct form in the sentence.)

trabajar	eschuchar	comer
tocar	llevar	ir
hablar	ser	beber
nadar	estar	cumplir

1. Mi mamá _____ paciente.

2. Yo _____ trece años.

3. Él _____ pantalones.

4. ¿_____ usted español?

5. Ellas _____ tristes.

6. Nosotros _____ en la piscina.

7. Ustedes _____ el refresco.

8. ¿ _____ tú la radio?

9. Ellos _____ al museo.

10. El señor Muñoz _____ en la oficina.

Clave de respuestas (Answer Key)

PAGE 3

51 cincuenta y uno (fifty-one)
52 cincuenta y dos (fifty-two)
53 cincuenta y tres (fifty-three)
54 cincuenta y cuatro (fifty-four)
55 cincuenta y cinco (fifty-five)
56 cincuenta y seis (fifty-six)
57 cincuenta y siete (fifty-seven)
58 cincuenta y ocho (fifty-eight)
59 cincuenta y nueve (fifty-nine)
60 sesenta (sixty)
61 sesenta y uno (sixty-one)
62 sesenta y dos (sixty-two)
63 sesenta y tres (sixty-three)
64 sesenta y cuatro (sixty-four)
65 sesenta y cinco (sixty-five)
66 sesenta y seis (sixty-six)

PAGE 4

67 sesenta y siete (sixty-seven)
68 sesenta y ocho (sixty-eight)
69 sesenta y nueve (sixty-nine)
70 setenta (seventy)
75 setenta y cinco (seventy-five)
80 ochenta (eighty)
85 ochenta y cinco (eighty-five)
90 noventa (ninety)
95 noventa y cinco (ninety-five)
100 cien (one hundred)
101 ciento uno (one hundred and one)
200 doscientos (two hundred)
201 doscientos uno (two hundred and one)
300 trescientos (three hundred)

PAGE 5

303 trescientos tres
   (three hundred and three)
400 cuatrocientos (four hundred)
404 cuatrocientos cuatro
   (four hundred and four)
500 quinientos (five hundred)
600 seiscientos (six hundred)
700 setecientos (seven hundred)
800 ochocientos (eight hundred)
900 novecientos (nine hundred)
1,000 mil (one thousand)
1,100 mil cien (one thousand, one hundred)
1,500 mil quinientos (one thousand,
   five hundred)
2,000 dos mil (two thousand)
10,000 diez mil (ten thousand)
100,000 cien mil (one hundred thousand)
1,000,000 un millón (one million)
2,000,000 dos millones (two million)

PAGE 6

sesenta y siete (sixty-seven)
ciento ochenta y uno (one hundred and
   eighty-one)
noventa y dos (ninety-two)
setenta y cuatro (seventy-four)
doscientos cuarenta y tres (two hundred and
   forty-three)
quinientos quince (five hundred and fifteen)
novecientos veintiséis (nine hundred and
   twenty-six)
trescientos cuatro (three hundred and four)
mil doscientos (one thousand, two hundred)
cuatro mil (four thousand)
quinientos mil ciento veintiséis (five hundred
   thousand, one hundred and twenty-six)
un millón ochocientos noventa y cuatro mil
   treinta y siete (one million, eight hundred
   ninety-four thousand, thirty-seven)
tres millones seiscientos mil doce (three
   million, six hundred thousand, twelve)
novecientos ochenta y siete mil seiscientos
   cincuenta y uno (nine hundred eighty-
   seven thousand, six hundred and fifty-one)

PAGE 7

393
54
8,007
1,101
713
2,011
1,000,014
902
500
15,000
1,000,600
10,022
730
14,000,000
5,500

PAGE 8

1. 531 + 914 = 1,445 / mil cuatrocientos
   cuarenta y cinco (one thousand, four
   hundred and forty-five)
2. 780 + 1,801 = 2,581 / dos mil quinientos
   ochenta y uno (two thousand, five
   hundred, eighty-one)
3. 4,600 − 406 = 4,194 / cuatro mil ciento
   noventa y cuatro (four thousand, one
   hundred, ninety-four
4. 10,117 + 1,570 = 8,547 / ocho mil
   quinientos cuarenta y siete (eight
   thousand, five hundred forty-seven)

Clave de respuestas (Answer Key)

PAGE 9

1492 mil cuatrocientos noventa y dos
(fourteen ninety-two)

1776 mil setecientos setenta y seis
(seventeen seventy-six)

1955 mil novecientos cincuenta y cinco
(nineteen fifty-five)

1812 mil ochocientos doce
(eighteen twelve)

1548 mil quinientos cuarenta y ocho
(fifteen forty-eight)

1637 mil seiscientos treinta y siete
(sixteen thirty-seven)

PAGE 11

canto (I sing)
cantas (you sing)
canta (you (formal)/he/she sings)
cantamos (we sing)
cantan (they sing)
llevo (I wear)
llevas (you wear)
lleva (you (formal)/he/she wears)
llevamos (we wear)
llevan (they wear)
estudio (I study)
estudias (you study)
estudia (you (formal)/he/she studies)
estudiamos (we study)
estudian (they study)

PAGE 12

los pantalones (the pants)
los pantalones cortos (the shorts)
la camisa (the shirt)
el suéter (the sweater)
el vestido (the dress)
la falda (the skirt)
el traje (the suit)
la corbata (the tie)
la camiseta (the T-shirt)
los zapatos (the shoes)
los calcetines (the socks)
las sandalias (the sandals)
el traje de baño (the swimsuit)
el abrigo (the coat)
la chaqueta (the jacket)

PAGE 13

1. Me gustan las camisetas. (I like T-shirts.)
2. Marcos lleva pantalones cortos. (Marcos wears shorts.)
3. Ana y María llevan vestidos. (Ana and María wear dresses.)
4. Nosotros llevamos trajes de baño. (We wear swimsuits.)
5. Yo compro la corbata. (I buy the tie.)
6. ¿Te gusta llevar sandalias? (Do you like to wear sandals?)
7. Ellos llevan pantalones. (They wear pants.)
8. Ellas compran faldas. (They buy skirts.)
9. Ella compra el abrigo. (She is buying the coat.)
10. Él lleva una chaqueta. (He wears a jacket.)
11. Me gustan los suéteres. (I like the sweaters.)

PAGE 14

1. Él mira el televisor. (He watches television.)
2. Yo estudio español. (I study Spanish.)
3. Ellas cantan una canción. (They sing a song.)

PAGE 15

4. Ella lleva un abrigo. (She wears a coat)
5. Yo toco el piano. (I play the piano.)
6. Nosotros escuchamos la radio. (We listen to the radio.)
7. Él compra una corbata. (He buys a tie.)
8. Yo deseo una manzana. (I want an apple.)
9. Él habla español. (He speaks Spanish.)
10. Ella prepara una torta. (She makes a cake.)

PAGE 16

2. Qué compra ella (What does she buy)
3. Qué habla él (What does he speak)
4. Qué llevas tú (What do you wear)
5. Qué tocan ustedes (What do you (plural) play)
6. Qué estudias tú (What do you study)
7. Qué visitan ustedes (What do you (plural) visit)
8. Qué escucha él (What does he listen to)

PAGE 17

9. Qué cantan ellos (What do they sing)
10. Qué miras tú (What do you watch)
11. Qué contestan ellas (What do they answer)
12. Qué te gusta (What do you like)
13. Qué estudia ella (What does she study)
14. Qué compran ustedes (What do you (plural) buy)
15. Qué toca ella (What does she play)

Clave de respuestas (Answer Key)

PAGE 18
1. ella habla ingles. (she speaks English.)
2. ellos no cantan bien. (they don't sing well.)
3. nosotros nadamos en la piscina. (we are swimming in the pool.)
4. ellas llevan vestidos. (they are wearing dresses.)

PAGE 19
5. yo no estudio historia. (I do not study history.)
6. ella prepara la comida. (she is preparing food.)
7. nosotros no miramos el televisor. (we do not watch television.)
8. yo escucho la radio. (I listen to the radio.)
9. él no baila bien. (he does not dance well.)
10. ella llora. (she cries.)
11. yo compro el suéter. (I buy the sweater.)

PAGE 20
1. Bailas tú mucho (Do you dance a lot)
2. Nada ella bien (Does she swim well)
3. Caminan ustedes (Do you (plural) walk)
4. Habla él francés (Does he speak French)
5. Escuchan ellas la radio (Do they listen to the radio)
6. Tocas tú la guitarra (Do you play the guitar)

PAGE 21
7. Visitan ustedes España (Do you visit Spain)
8. Lleva ella un abrigo (Does she wear a coat)
9. Estudias tú ciencias (Do you study science)
10. Bailan ellos (Do they dance)
11. Hablas tú español (Do you speak Spanish)
12. Mira él el televisor (Does he watch television.)

PAGE 22
1. Sí, yo hablo ingles. (Yes, I speak English.)
2. Él habla español. (He speaks Spanish.)
3. No, ellas no miran el televisor. (No, they do not watch television.)
4. Me gustan las palomitas. (I like popcorn.)
5. Sí, yo nado. (Yes, I am swimming.)

PAGE 23
6. Sí, nosotros escuchamos la radio. (Yes, we listen to the radio.)
7. No, ella no llora. (No, she does not cry.)
8. Yo toco el piano. (I play the piano.)
9. Sí, ellas cantan. (Yes, they sing.)
10. Sí, ellos saludan. (Yes, they greet.)
11. Ella estudia español. (She studies Spanish.)

PAGE 24
1. seria (serious) (feminine, singular)
2. graciosa (funny) (feminine, singular)

PAGE 25
3. morena (dark-haired) (feminine, singular)
4. rubia (blond) (feminine)
5. vieja (old) (feminine, singular)
6. tímida (shy) (feminine, singular)
7. pequeña (small) (feminine, singular)
8. simpática (nice) (feminine, singular)
9. antipática (not nice, mean) (feminine, singular)

PAGE 27
1. inteligente (intelligent)
2. joven (young)
3. grande (big)
4. serio (serious) (masculine)
5. morena (dark-haired) (feminine)
6. inocente (innocent)
7. paciente (patient)
8. independiente (independent)
9. bajo (short) (masculine)
10. rubia (blond) (feminine)
11. tímido (shy) (masculine)
12. interesante (interesting)
13. excelente (excellent)
14. difícil (hard)
15. grande (big)
16. graciosa (funny) (feminine)

PAGE 29
1. pequeñas (small) (feminine, plural)
2. interesantes (interesting) (plural)
3. tímidos (shy) (masculine, plural)
4. inocentes (innocent) (plural)
5. difíciles (difficult) (plural)
6. aburridas (boring) (feminine, plural)
7. bonitas (pretty) (feminine, plural)
8. excelentes (excellent) (plural)
9. graciosas (funny) (feminine, plural)
10. grandes (big) (plural)
11. simpáticos (nice) (masculine, plural)
12. impacientes (impatient) (plural)

Clave de respuestas (Answer Key)

PAGE 30
1. grande (big)
2. bajo (short) (masculine, singular)
3. rubia (blond) (feminine, singular)
4. aburrida (boring) (feminine, singular)
5. pequeña (small) (feminine, singular)
6. excelente (excellent) (singular)
7. alto (tall) (masculine, singular)
8. simpáticas (nice) (feminine, plural)
9. antipáticos (mean) (masculine, plural)
10. vieja (old) (feminine, singular)
11. gracioso (funny) (masculine, singular)
12. moreno (dark-haired) (masculine, singular)

PAGE 31
13. joven (young) (singular)
14. simpática (nice) (feminine, singular)
15. inteligentes (smart) (plural)
16. difícil (difficult) (singular)
17. inocentes (innocent) (plural)
18. fáciles (easy) (plural)
19. paciente (patient) (singular)
20. inteligente (smart) (singular)
21. grandes (big) (plural)
22. simpático (nice) (masculine, singular)
23. altas (tall) (feminine, plural)
24. rubio (blond) (masculine, singular)

PAGE 32
1. soy alto/alta (I am tall)
2. eres alta (you are tall) (feminine, familiar)
3. es alto (you are tall) (masculine, formal)
4. es alto (he is tall)
5. es alta (she is tall)
6. somos altos (we are tall) (masculine)
7. somos altas (we are tall) (feminine)
8. son altos (you are tall) (masculine, plural)
9. son altos (they are tall) (masculine, plural)
10. son altas (they are tall) (feminine, plural)

PAGE 33
1. soy bajo/a (I am short)
2. eres bajo (you are short) (masculine, singular)
3. es baja (she is short)
4. somos bajos (we are short) (masculine, plural)
5. son bajos (you are short) (masculine, plural)
6. son bajas (you are short) (feminine, plural)

1. eres inteligente (you are intelligent) (singular)
2. son inteligentes (they are intelligent)
3. somos inteligentes (we are intelligent)
4. soy inteligente (I am intelligent)
5. son inteligentes (you are intelligent) (plural)
6. es inteligente (he is intelligent)
7. son inteligentes (they are intelligent)
8. es inteligente (you are intelligent) (formal)

PAGE 34
1. Mónica es inteligente. Mónica es simpática. (Mónica is smart. Mónica is nice)
2. Roberto es inocente. Roberto es alto. (Roberto is innocent. Roberto is tall.)
3. Ana y María son pacientes. Ana y María son rubias. (Ana and María are patient. Ana and María are blond.)
4. Marcos y Pablo son jóvenes. Marcos y Pablo son impacientes. (Marcos and Pablo are young. Marcos and Pablo are impatient.)
5. Pedro y Rosita son bajos. Pedro y Rosita son morenos. (Pedro and Rosita are short. Pedro and Rosita are dark-haired.)

PAGE 35
6. Los libros son fáciles. Los libros son interesantes. (The books are easy. The books are interesting.)
7. Nosotros somos graciosos. Nosotros somos independientes. (We are funny. We are independent.)
8. Yo soy alta. Yo soy simpática. (I am tall. I am nice.)
9. La chica es antipática. La chica es aburrida. (The girl is mean. The girl is boring.)
10. Las casas son bonitas. Las casas son pequeñas. (The houses are pretty. The houses are small.)

PAGE 36
1. Sí, ella es estricta. (She is strict.)
2. No, yo no soy bajo. Yo soy alto. (No, I am not short. I am tall.)

Clave de respuestas (Answer Key)

PAGE 37

3. Sí, ellos son graciosos.
   (Yes, they are funny.)
4. Sí, nosotros somos pacientes.
   (Yes, we are patient.)
5. No, ella no es morena. Ella es rubia. (No, she is not dark-haired. She is blond.)
6. No, el libro no es interesante. El libro es aburrido. (No, the book is not interesting. The book is boring.)
7. No, él no es viejo. Él es joven. (No, he is not old. He is young.)
8. No, ella no es simpática. Ella es antipática. (No, she is not nice. She is mean.)

PAGE 40

1. soy artista (am an artist)
2. es mecánico (is a mechanic) (masculine)
3. somos periodistas (are journalists)
4. es enfermera (is a nurse) (feminine)
5. es músico (is a musician) (masculine)

PAGE 41

6. es cantante (is a singer)
7. es escritor (is a writer) (masculine)
8. es doctora (is a doctor) (feminine)
9. es piloto (is a pilot) (masculine)
10. es cocinero (is a cook) (masculine)
11. es dentista (is a dentist)
12. eres fotógrafo/a (are a photographer)
13. son abogados (are lawyers) (masculine, plural)
14. es bailarín (is a dancer) (masculine)
15. es profesora (is a teacher) (feminine)

PAGE 42

Es la una. (It's one.)
Son las dos. (It's two.)
Son las tres. (It's three.)
Son las cuatro. (It's four.)

PAGE 43

Es mediodía. (It's midday.)
Es medianoche. (It's midnight.)
Son las cinco y cinco. (It's five after five.)
Son las ocho y cuarto. (It's eight fifteen.)
Son las diez y veinticinco. (It's ten twenty-five.)

PAGE 44

Son las nueve y media. (It's nine thirty.)
Son las diez menos veinte. (It's nine forty.)
Son las diez menos cuarto. (It's quarter to ten.)
Son las diez menos diez. (It's ten to ten.)
Son las diez menos cinco. (It's five to ten.)

PAGE 45

Son las seis. (It's six.)
Son las once y cuarto. (It's eleven fifteen.)
Es la una y media. (It's one thirty.)
Son las tres menos cuarto. (It's quarter to three.)
Son las siete y veinte. (It's seven twenty.)
Son las cuatro menos cinco. (It's five to four.)
Son las ocho y veinticinco. (It's eight twenty-five.)

PAGE 47

1. La clase es a las nueve de la mañana. (The class is at nine in the morning.)
2. El almuerzo es a las once y veinte de la mañana. (Lunch is at eleven twenty in the morning.)
3. La clase es a las diez y veinte de la mañana. (The class is at ten twenty in the morning.)
4. La clase es a las doce y media de la tarde. (The class is at twelve thirty in the afternoon.)
5. El recreo es a las diez de la mañana. (Recess is at ten in the morning.)
6. La clase es a la una y media de la tarde. (The class is at one thirty in the afternoon.)
7. La clase es a las ocho de la mañana. (The class is at eight in the morning.)
8. Las clases terminan a las dos y veinticinco de la tarde. (The classes finish at two twenty-five in the afternoon.)

PAGE 49

1. estamos	(we are)
2. están	(they are)
3. estoy	(I am)
4. estás	(are you)
5. está	(is)

1. es	(she is)
2. somos	(we are)
3. están	(they are)
4. es	(is)
5. está	(is)
6. estoy	(I am)
7. estás	(you are)
8. están	(they are)

Clave de respuestas (Answer Key)

PAGE 50

Está soleado.	(It's sunny.)
Está nublado.	(It's cloudy.)
Está lluvioso.	(It's rainy.)
Está helado.	(It's frosty.)
Está nevado.	(It's snowy.)
Está despejado.	(It's clear.)
Está fresco.	(It's cool.)
Está caluroso.	(It's warm.)

PAGE 51

1. Está nevado.	(It's snowy.)
2. Está caluroso.	(It's warm.)
3. Está lluvioso.	(It's rainy.)
4. Está helado.	(It's frosty.)
5. Está nublado.	(It's cloudy.)
6. Está soleado.	(It's sunny.)
7. Está despejado.	(It's clear.)
8. Está fresco.	(It's cool.)

PAGE 52

en el campo	(at the country)
en la ciudad	(at the city)
en la escuela	(at school)
en el restaurante	(at the restaurant)
en la playa	(at the beach)
en el aeropuerto	(at the airport)

PAGE 53

en la piscina	(at the pool)
en la casa	(at home)
en el cine	(at the movies)
en la oficina	(at the office)
en España	(in Spain)
en el teatro	(at the theater)
en los Estados Unidos	(in United States)
en México	(in Mexico)

PAGE 54

1. Ella está en la escuela. (She is at school.)
2. Él está en la piscina. (He is in the pool.)
3. Yo estoy en la casa. (I am at the house.)
4. Ellos están en el restaurante. (They are at the restaurant.)
5. Yo estoy en la oficina. (I am at the office.)
6. Nosotros estamos en el cine. (We are at the movies.)

PAGE 55

7. Ellos caminan en la playa. (They are walking on the beach.)
8. Ella trabaja en la oficina. (She works in the office.)
9. Ellos están en los Estados Unidos. (They are in the United States.)
10. Yo estudio en la casa. (I study at home.)
11. Ellos están en el teatro. (They are at the theater.)
12. El avión está en el aeropuerto. (The plane is at the airport.)

PAGE 56

1. Yo voy a la escuela. (I go to school.)
2. Ella va al parque. (She goes to the park.)

PAGE 57

3. Ellos van a la playa. (They go to the beach.)
4. Nosotros/as vamos a la estación. (We go to the station.)
5. Ellos van al hotel. (They go to the hotel.)
6. Yo voy al café. (I go to the café.)
7. Él va al aeropuerto. (He goes to the airport.)
8. Ella va al cine. (She goes to the movies.)

PAGE 58

1. Lola va a cantar mañana. (Lola is going to sing tomorrow.)
2. Cristina y Ana van a bailar. (Cristina and Ana are going to dance.)
3. Los chicos van a estudiar. (The kids are going to study.)
4. Yo voy a caminar mañana. (I am going to walk tomorrow.)
5. Nosotras vamos a contestar. (We are going to answer.)
6. Las hermanas van a visitar mañana. (The sisters are going to visit tomorrow.)
7. Manuel va a trabajar mañana. (Manuel is going to work tomorrow.)

Clave de respuestas (Answer Key)

PAGE 59
1. yo voy a estudiar mañana. (I am going to study tomorrow.)
2. ellas van a llorar. (they are going to cry.)
3. nosotros no vamos a hablar en clase. (we are not going to talk in class.)
4. ella va a escuchar. (she is going to listen.)
5. él no va a mirar el televisor. (he is not going to watch television.)
6. yo no voy a comprar ropa. (I am not going to buy clothes.)
7. yo voy a nadar mañana. (I am going to swim tomorrow.)

PAGE 61
com
como (I eat)
comes (you eat)
come (you (formal)/he/she eats)
comemos (we eat)
comen (they eat)
1. bebemos (we drink)
2. vende (she sells)
3. aprenden (they learn)
4. corre (he runs)
5. comprenden (you (plural) understand)
6. debo (I owe)
7. comes (you eat)
8. sabe (she knows)
9. lee (you (formal) read)
10. bebo (I drink)

PAGE 63
escrib
escribo (I write)
escribes (you write)
escribe (you (formal)/he/she writes)
escribimos (we write)
escriben (they write)
1. decide (does not decide)
2. Viven (Do you live)
3. abre (it opens)
4. recibo (I receive)
5. asistimos (we attend)
6. cumple (he turns)
7. Subes (Do you go up)
8. escribe (she writes)
9. Abre (Do you (formal) open)
10. cumplen (they turn)

PAGE 64
¡Canta!	(Sing!)
¡Habla español!	(Speak Spanish!)
¡Mira el televisor!	(Watch television!)
¡Nada!	(Swim!)
¡Come!	(Eat!)
¡Escucha!	(Listen!)
¡Corre!	(Run!)
¡Contesta!	(Answer!)

PAGE 65
¡Cante!	(Sing!)
¡Hable español!	(Speak Spanish!)
¡Mire el televisor!	(Watch television!)
¡Nade!	(Swim!)
¡Coma!	(Eat!)
¡Escuche!	(Listen!)
¡Corra!	(Run!)
¡Conteste!	(Answer!)

PAGE 66
1. Ella vive en Santiago. (She lives in Santiago.)
2. No, ella es de Chile. (No, she is from Chile.)
3. Le gustan las clases de geografía y de ingles. (She likes the geography and English class.)
4. Le gusta llevar una camiseta y jeans. (She likes to wear a T-shirt and jeans.)
5. No, ella habla español y habla inglés. (No, she speaks Spanish and English.)

PAGE 67
1. Si, él es muy deportivo. (Yes, he is very sporty.)
2. No, él es alto y moreno. (No, he is tall and dark haired.)
3. No, él no estudia con sus amigos. (No, he does not study with his friends.)
4. Si, le gusta la escuela. (Yes, he likes school.)

Clave de respuestas (Answer Key)

PAGE 68
1. No, ella es de España. (No, she is from Spain.)
2. No, Carlos es de los Estados Unidos. (No, Carlos is from the United States.)

PAGE 69
3. Carlos es bajo, rubio y sincero. (Carlos is short, blond, and sincere.)
4. Sí, le gustan los deportes. (Yes, he likes sports.)
5. Sí, le gustan también los deportes. (Yes, she likes sports too.)
6. No, no les gusta correr. (No, they don't like to run.)
7. La escuela está en Barcelona. (The school is in Barcelona.)
8. La escuela está en Tarragona. (The school is in Tarragona.)
9. Sí, le gusta la historia. (Yes, she likes history.)
10. Sí, ellos son inteligentes. (Yes, they are intelligent.)

PAGE 70
Across
5. dónde (where)
6. abrigo (coat)
7. voy (I am going)
8. caminar (to walk)
10. español (Spanish)
11. baja (short) (feminine, singular)
13. estoy (I am)
14. viejo (old) (masculine, singular)
16. simpático (nice) (masculine, singular)
18. escribes (you write)

Down
1. teatro (theater)
2. vivir (to live)
3. soy (I am)
4. piscina (pool)
5. doscientos (two hundred)
9. piloto (pilot)
12. somos (we are)
15. falda (skirt)
17. cien (one hundred)
19. ir (to go)

PAGE 71
1. ser (to be)
2. aburrido (boring) (masculine, singular)
3. llorar (to cry)
4. fácil (easy) (singular)
5. obreros (factory worker) (masculine, plural)
6. seria (serious) (feminine, singular)
7. saludar (to greet)
8. periodista (journalist) (singular)
9. abogados (lawyer) (masculine, plural)
10. medianoche (midnight)
11. enfermera (nurse) (feminine, singular)
12. abrir (to open)
13. leer (to read)
14. gracioso (funny) (masculine, singular)
15. sandalias (sandals)
16. zapatos (shoes)
17. sesenta (sixty)
18. corbata (tie)
19. qué (what)
20. trabajar (to work)

PAGE 72
1. es (she is)
2. cumplo (I turn)
3. lleva (he wears)
4. Habla (Do you (formal) talk)
5. están (they are)
6. nadamos (we swim)
7. beben (they drink)
8. Escuchas (Do you hear)
9. van (they go)
10. trabaja (he works)